Good
Architecture

enhances all
of our lives.

Patrick Killen
oct. 12

THE MODERN CALIFORNIAN
BEACH HOUSE

PATRICK KILLEN

THE MODERN CALIFORNIAN

BEACH HOUSE

images
Publishing

Published in Australia in 2012 by
The Images Publishing Group Pty Ltd
ABN 89 059 734 431
6 Bastow Place, Mulgrave, Victoria 3170, Australia
Tel: +61 3 9561 5544 Fax: +61 3 9561 4860
books@imagespublishing.com
www.imagespublishing.com

National Library of Australia Cataloguing-in-Publication entry
Author: Killen, Patrick with Russell Abraham.
Title: The modern Californian beach house / Patrick Killen.
ISBN: 9781864704594 (hbk.)
Subjects: Architecture, Modern–21st century–California.
                 Architecture, Modern–20th century–California.
                 Architecture, Domestic–California.
                 Architecture and climate–California.
                 Architecture–American influences.
Edited by: Debbie Ball
Dewey Number: 720.9794

Designed by The Graphic Image Studio Pty Ltd, Mulgrave, Australia
www.tgis.com.au

Pre-publishing services by Mission Productions Limited, Hong Kong

Printed by Everbest Printing Co. Ltd., in Hong Kong/China on 150gsm Quatro silk
matt paper

IMAGES has included on its website a page for special notices in relation to this
and our other publications. Please visit www.imagespublishing.com.

CONTENTS

THE MODERN CALIFORNIA BEACH HOU

Physically, Los Angeles (L.A.) is a vast metropolis that stretches from the shores of the Pacific Ocean to the foothills of the San Gabriel and Tehachapi Mountains to the edges of the Mojave Desert. It is spanned by an unparalleled freeway system that is the envy of the world and the object of local derision. At times, driving down the I-10 freeway, a ten-lane ribbon of concrete that stretches from the ocean to the desert, it can be difficult to tell if you are in Culver City or Claremont. Along with New York, Tokyo and London, Los Angeles is one of the world's great cities. In the United States, its metropolitan population is second only to New York and among the top 10 cities worldwide. But more importantly, Los Angeles is an intricate patchwork of small towns, neighborhoods and bustling ethnic communities that give the city a uniquely urbane and ever-changing character. Los Angeles is a financial center, a center for international trade, a high-tech and aerospace manufacturing center and most significantly, the center of the world's film industry. Its native film, television, and music industries produce much of the world's entertainment. Television dramas produced decades ago are still broadcast in close to a hundred countries and in as many languages. One in six people who live in Los Angeles work in some creative field as actors, writers, musicians, filmmakers, directors; making it the largest concentration of artists and creative people in the world.

THE WORKS OF STUDIO 9ONE2

Seventy years ago, Los Angeles was a mid-sized American city surrounded by two score of smaller towns whose economies were based on agriculture, petroleum extraction and light manufacturing. On the city's western edge were a series of small beach towns that collectively constituted the single greatest stretch of urban beachfront in the world. A post World War II building boom and access to water, caused the City of Los Angeles to grow from its center and eclipse most of its surrounding towns. The end result is today's mega-city limited only by mountains and oceans.

In the early 1900s, the lands that lined the Pacific shores of Los Angeles County were incorporated as beach towns. From Malibu in the north to Huntington Beach in the south, the coastal towns were the locus of primary agricultural and fishing industries. Many were connected to Los Angeles proper by railway lines and later streetcars. Developers and beach town boosters encouraged development by building fishing piers, railway lines and later, entertainment venues so that city people would take the hour plus train ride from the city to visit the ocean for the day. Starting in the 1920s, the land immediately facing the beaches was subdivided into small lots appropriate for inexpensive housing for cannery workers, fishermen and the occasional city family who wanted a seaside weekend home. Some towns like Venice Beach and Manhattan Beach laid out their towns in a pedestrian-friendly manner, with the primary street being a pedestrian only path and automobile access limited to a rear alley. The net result was a quaint, compact, urban landscape very different from the suburban sprawl of surrounding Los Angeles.

It was here that a unique community of fishermen, cannery workers, actors, musicians, and simple Angelinos looking for a weekend getaway, built some of the most unique, and colorful communities in all of Southern California. LA's beach towns became a local treasure known mostly to other Angelinos. Their coffee houses became way stations for the Beat poets and writers of the 1950s and 1960s. Their bars became the hot West Coast venues for the bebop jazz scene of the same era.

Today, LA.'s beach culture has been popularized worldwide in both song and film. "Wish they all could be Californian Girls" still rings in the head of many a man of a certain age. However, the beach town sub-culture that generated this Beach Boys' song and an entire musical genre is both home grown and uniquely Southern Californian. The carefree and creative lifestyle that most people identify with, California has its origins in the beach towns of Los Angeles.

Patrick John Killen, from Blue-collar to No Collar

Patrick John Killen grew up in the blue-collar steel towns of Eastern Ohio, not far from Youngstown. Born of Irish and Italian heritage, he attended 12 years of parochial schools. Naturally a left-hander, his Roman Catholic nun teachers admonished him until he learned to write with his right hand. This coercion aggravated a natural dyslexic tendency and caused the young Killen to at times write upside and backwards. School was not fun. He found refuge in art, first in color paper montages and later in making large, Mondrian like, constructions from balsa wood. As a teenager he worked summers with his dad as a sheet metal worker. This galvanized his love for all things metal that is prominently displayed in much of his architecture today. He also worked in an aluminum plant where he sparked a six-week wildcat strike over working conditions.

Later Killen worked in a steel mill as a slag-breaker, suspended on a harness and armed with only a hard hat, mask and hammer, his job was to chip away the slag that coated the red hot steel ingots as they slowly rolled out of the blast furnace. The young Killen quickly figured out that life in the steel mills of Youngstown was not for him. In his freshman year in high school his family ventured to the World's Fair in Montreal, Canada where for the first time he was exposed to a collection of work of the world's finest architects of the day. Killen was transfixed. Whoever these people were who created these magnificent structures, he vowed to be one of them.

Whatever his issues with writing and language, he graduated from high school with grades good enough to get into Kent State University, one of Ohio's leading universities, majoring in architecture. Killen excelled, graduating at the top of his class. His excellent college work enabled him to join a well-known firm just out of school. He worked with this Cleveland firm for a few years until he decided in 1980 it was time to move west. For many people in the United States, California was the personification of the utopian dream perpetuated by a relentless media machine in Los Angeles, a cultural magnate with a wide-reaching draw.

He applied to a variety of West Coast firms and was offered jobs by most of them. Killen ultimately took a position with Skidmore, Owings and Merrill (SOM), a safer bet at the time. At Skidmore, he worked on the Universal Amphitheater, the Pershing Square Jewelry Mart and a variety of office towers. Upon leaving SOM he was introduced to his replacement, Steven Kanner, who would also eventually leave SOM to become a partner at Kanner Architects, a family firm, that he would develop into one of Los Angeles' most highly regarded modernist

architectural firms. Killen started his own firm in Redondo Beach in 1982. In 1987 he decided to move to the warehouse district of downtown Los Angeles and rename his firm, Architrave. Here, he took on larger institutional and commercial projects including a regional Olympic training swimming facility at the Rosebowl Park for the City of Pasadena. Living by the ocean and commuting to downtown Los Angeles soon lost its appeal. In 1992 he closed Architrave and moved his practice back to the beach and renamed it Studio 9one2, the eponymous address of his storefront Manhattan Beach office. In 1993 he hired Howard Crabtree, a recent graduate, to join him in his practice. Howard has been there ever since overseeing many of the technical aspects of the firm's designs. Killen refers to Crabtree as "the person who makes everything work."

Beach Life Meets Modernism

By the 1980s L.A.'s beach communities were a stewing pot of cultural anomalies. Out of work actors lived next door to retirees and drug dealers. The beach towns were both alluring and a bit scary. The elegance of an earlier time stood next to contemporary decay. Architecturally, the towns were a crazy quilt of fantasy structures all built on postage stamp sized lots wedged together in a dense pattern, laid out generations earlier, and very different from the rest of LA. The beach towns offered Angelinos fresh air, quaint neighborhoods and the opportunity to buy an inexpensive property, and rebuild it into something desirable. Individuals and families looking for a real estate bargain and possessing the desire to make an architectural statement, found the beach towns appealing. It was in this environment of social and economic unrest that Patrick Killen opened his beachfront studio and introduced high style Modernism to the beach towns of Los Angeles. Killen was not the first Modernist to build at the beach. A generation earlier, the likes of Rudolph Schindler, Craig Ellwood and Charles Eames had built at or near the beach. However, most of their projects were free-standing buildings on large lots, not urban infill. Killen's first beach house was a remodel completed in 1984. At the time, very few architects were attempting to create serious Modern Design here. With its mild and dry climate, the beach towns of Southern California were the perfect environment for "The International Style", later known simply as "Modernism." Developed mostly in Germany in the early 20th Century, Modernism was popularized by Southern California architects in the 1950s and 1960s, however was used mostly in commercial and institutional projects. Starting in the mid-1980s, Killen and a very small handful of architects re-introduced the Modern Style as a beach house paradigm.

In 1991 Killen was approached by a couple that owned an ocean-front property in Manhattan Beach, who were looking for a beach house that was avant-garde. Killen's earlier work at the beach had given his clients confidence that Killen could produce what they desired. As with all beachfront lots, the size and setback requirements presented a constrained building envelope. Killen's solution was to use the lifeguard stands, just yards away, as a design inspiration. He took the lifeguard stand's 78 degree windows and mimicked that shape in a canted wall that bifurcated the front elevation. Working from either side of this wall, Killen hung balconies and bays that projected rakishly toward the ocean. Internally, the wall was repeated in art glass and stainless steel separating the atrium from the dining room. Taking the 78 degree theme to the plan

level, Killen rotated the entire structure to a 12 degree offset from the property lines and placed third-story balconies and bays at the same rotation. Using simple but durable materials, glass, stainless steel and stucco, Killen created an eye-popping, exuberant, Modernist building in a sea of sameness. With awards and press to follow, Killen's Shearin House established Modernism as a viable architectural motif on the western edge of Los Angeles.

Killen's work today, has become a 21st-Century extrapolation of the mid-Century Southern California Modernists, exemplified by Eames and Ellwood. He is adamant in his commitment to Modernism. He says, "It is the architecture of our time and should not be ignored." His work is both disciplined and filled with unalloyed fun. Killen is not afraid to mix intense color into his work; nor is he locked into a rigid grid or coordinate system. Each of his houses is unique, designed from the ground up to suit the individual needs of his eclectic clientele. The mold is always broken before a new house is started. Stucco clad forms are juxtaposed with cantilevered decks and two-story walls of glass. Concrete block walls find their way from outside structure to interiors, becoming decorative surfaces. Ceramic-tile sheathing flows seamlessly from outside to inside. Southern California's exceptionally mild climate allows Killen to bring the outside inside: with lush internal courtyards, rooms with roll-away walls, and pools that wrap half way around the house.

All of Killen's work evokes an exuberance that is uniquely Southern Californian. It pushes the perceived limits of design a notch or two each time and creates a paradigm that makes complete sense for California. Killen's 139 Hermosa Beach Boulevard house exemplifies his sense of humor and design prowess. Using the Apple iPod as an inspiration, Killen took the tubular iPod form, covered it in blue ceramic tile and placed it on a horizontal cradle painted bright green. Sitting on a busy commercial street on one side and fronting a car access street and the ocean on the other, the house is both shocking and appropriate for its beachfront location. The commercial street side is a first floor retail space and the blue tube above is a two-story condo that runs the length of the property. The western end of the tube is cut away to become a two-story deck with ocean views. The end result is sublime.

Patrick John Killen migrated to the beaches of Southern California to find solace. What he found instead, was a client base willing to stretch the limits of Modern Architecture. His response was to create one of the most inspired portfolios of any regional architect of the era.

Russell Abraham
Los Angeles,
the City of the Queen of the Angels

(2) Arroyo
Sequit Park

(5) Dunz
Park

(6) Ramirez
Canyon
Reservations

Santa *Monica* *Mountains*

(22) Topanga
Canyon
Park
Uplands

(25) Castellammare
Beach

(26) Santa
Ynez
Beach

(13) Pacific
Malibu
Park

(10) Escondido
Canyon
Mouth

(17) Carbon
Beyond
Las Flores
Beach

(19) East
Las
Flores
Beach

(1) Sequit
Beach

(3) Nicolas and
Encinal Beaches
and Bluffs

(4) Zuma
Beach

Malibu

(11) Corral
Beaches

(16) East
Carbon
Beach

(20) Pena
Canyon
Beach

(23 & 24)
Topanga
Beach

(30) Santa
Monica
Canyon
Beach

(9) Escondido
Beach

(12) Malibu
Beaches
and Plains

(14) Malibu
Slough
and East
Beach

(21) Tuna
Canyon
Beach

(7) Dume
Point
Shore

(8) Ramirez
Beach
and Bluffs

Point
Dume

(18) Las
Flores
Delta

(15) West
Carbon
Beach

(33 & 34) Beach Clubs

(39 & 40) Santa Monica Pier
and Beaches to Lick Pier

(41 & 42) Lick Pier to Del Rey
Pier through Venice

Santa *Monica* *Bay*

(49, 50 & 51)
El Segundo and
Angeles County

(52 & 53) Co
Bea

(54

Pacific *Ocean*

PROJECTS

Some fortunes take a generation to create, others just an immediate and advantageous draw of cards. Agave House in Hermosa Beach is a product of the latter. A small group of professional card players decided to pool some of their profits and build a weekend retreat next to the ocean, far away from the bright lights of Las Vegas. They wanted a fun, distinctive house that they could find both solitude and entertain their broad spectrum of guests. The lot they bought was on a busy corner, one city block from the beach. Studio 9one2's task was to pack a lot of house into a 60 feet x 60 feet lot and provide some visual and auditory separation from the street. Killen saw this as a "Rubik's cube" type challenge.

In order to provide separation from the busy street, Studio 9one2 created a three-story high screen wall with large cutouts and planters filled with Blue Agaves. The cutouts were strategically positioned in front of windows, one in the living room and one in the master bedroom. Illuminated at night, these suspended metal planters read as paintings on the wall of the inside space that they served; giving a garden like feel to those spaces.

Killen articulated the main entrance with a three-story high window wall that framed the staircase and then wrapped 90 degrees at the top to become part of the third floor. Running down the middle of the third floor, this glass floor insert divided the building into

Opposite: Detail of screen wall with Agave planters

Above: Primary street elevation

A HOUSE OF CARDS IN HERMOSA BEACH

AGAVE HOUSE

two halves. Like many of Studio 9one2 projects, the entertaining floor was on the top level, to take in the ocean views. On this level, Killen popped out a small deck next to the dining room and topped it with a cantilevered roof projection that helped define a sense of personal space on this very tight lot. Ninety-degrees mitered glass windows on the upper levels framed ocean views.

Projected roof soffits, "Zincalume" metal panels and dark-wood wing walls and panels, were combined in unique ways to give this house a sense of visual excitement on a busy Hermosa Beach corner.

AGAVE HOUSE

Opposite: Family room

Above: View of kitchen from living room

Following Pages: Overall view of primary entertainment spaces at third floor

19

AGAVE HOUSE

AJIR-BL

The clients, of this dramatic infill house, were a young professional couple with school-age children; who were drawn to live next to the ocean. They said they wanted to both "see and taste the ocean." They bought an older bungalow on a quiet pedestrian street, with the intent of building a modern house that would suit their lifestyle. They interviewed several architectural firms, who had a modern design focus; hoping to find someone who could realize their vision of a versatile indoor-outdoor living space. They chose Killen for both his design prowess and enthusiasm.

Killen's design solution created a building with a strong collection of vertical elements and volumes of brightly accented colors, that gave it a "Mondrian-like" appearance. Killen defined the main circulation space with a giant pink L-shaped form. The staircase, placed against a solid external bearing wall, had glass treads and floor to ceiling windows at the landings, that kept it light and inviting.

The client says, "We wanted the downstairs space to accommodate creativity in all forms; entertain groups of people; to paint or sculpt; spill drinks while watching the Super Bowl; extend out onto the pedestrian street, to open the house to guests." Killen gave shape to that desire; he created a ground floor with a recessed courtyard; a roll-up, glazed, garage door; which allowed the family to greet their guests and entertain on multiple levels at once. This courtyard also became an outdoor extension of the children's playroom. One of

Opposite: Evening view from dining room

Above: Rear of building at garage access from alley

MONDRIAN GOES TO THE BEACH

UME HOUSE

AJIR-BLUME HOUSE

Opposite Left: Entry façade from pedestrian walk-street with produce garden in foreground
Opposite Above Right: Evening view of entry façade and garden
Opposite Below Right: Detail of form over entry

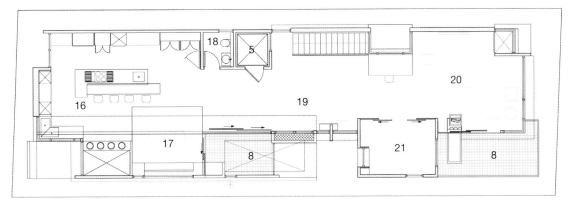

Second floor

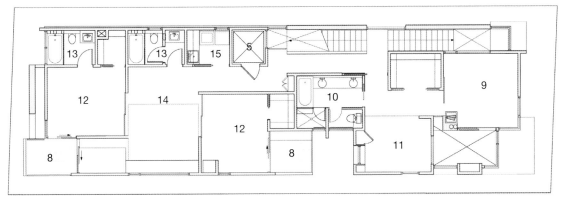

First floor

1   Entry
2   Recreation room
3   Guest bathroom
4   Garage
5   Elevator
6   Courtyard
7   Frontyard
8   Deck
9   Master bedroom
10 Master bathroom
11 Gym
12 Bedroom
13 Bathroom
14 Playroom
15 Laundry
16 Kitchen
17 Dining
18 Powder room
19 Sitting area
20 Living room
21 Sound room

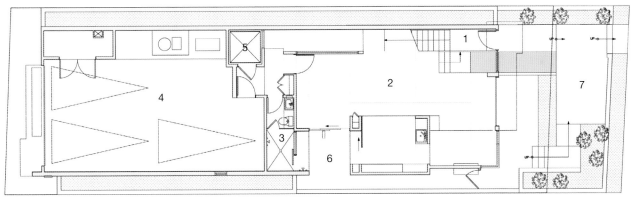

Basement

25

the courtyard's more unique features was a large rectangular Japanese Koi pond that extended into the children's playroom, where it was glazed on three sides for easy fish viewing.

By incorporating large glass plates at various spots in the floor, the mother could keep an eye on her children from one floor away. The glass floor also brought copious amounts of daylight into the lower levels of the house. On the western façade, large decks and rollaway glass window walls opened onto magnificent ocean views and filled the interiors with intense daylight.

The clients wanted a few special places in the house, where the children could do art and they could play music together. On the northern side of the house, Killen designed a three-story rectangular tower, which he cladded in Carrera Marble inside and out. The tower enclosed three creative spaces: an art room, an office and a music room on sequential floors. Killen saw the marble as having a symbolic significance, which reminded us that this was the same stone that built Rome.

The master suite on the second level had a loft-like ambience and opened to the staircase on one side and the kids' playroom below. Privacy is achieved through a heavy velvet theater curtain that is drawn in a circle around the bed.

Killen used intersecting rectangular volumes both horizontally and vertically that created a delightful and unique sense of play and lightness on a very constricted site. These forms, along with L-shaped projections, fused the minimalist lines into a distinctive composition that makes a strong, but joyful statement.

AJIR-BLUME HOUSE

Opposite: Koi pond at entry with roll-up door access to front yard

Right: Glass staircase

Below: Sitting area at glass floor with views to children's play space below
Right: Kitchen with sitting area

Our client wanted to build a beach house that would have the feeling of an artist's loft, while still retaining old-world charm of beach bungalows from a hundred years ago. This walk-street residence, designed for a 30 feet x 90 feet interior beach lot, integrates traditional materials and a very contemporary design to produce this unconventional and dramatic beach house.

The house is a collection of very simple rectangular volumes capped by a shed roof with a deep overhang. Killen mixes concrete block, stucco and distinctive asphalt shingles to frame and sheath the building. The blue asphalt shingle siding celebrates an era of bungalow style houses built at the turn of the last century, adding color and valuable texture to the home. In stark contrast to the building's metal and stucco elements, the shingles provide a vibrant color, while also defining levels and volumes. An exposed concrete block, an earthy element, grounds the structure. The pier-like columns, seen both inside and out at the entry, also provide a sense of permanence to the house. Windows with intermediate mullions resemble older, traditional multi-paned windows. This retro detail adds strength to the loft look. The open wood decks and wood railings on the third floor recall a time when these materials created decks and porches for the residents to welcome neighbors. Here they create an

Opposite: View into courtyard

Above Left: Rear façade at vehicular-access alley
Above Right: Entry façade off pedestrian-access walk-street

BORROWING FROM THE PAST AND REACHING INTO THE FUTURE

LMO HOUSE

ANSELMO HOUSE

inside / outside deck extending the space at the third level towards the beach.

The entry and children's bedrooms open to a courtyard at the center of the home creating a large play space. This further provides an extension of indoor / outdoor interaction. By notching the building in the center at all three floors, a third level deck and windows facing north and south can receive sunlight most of the year. The cutout also allows for views from the inner most portions of the house as well as reduces the mass of the building. The main stair rises out of the two-story entry space. The liberal use of steel and wood on the stairs creates a feeling of casual yet enduring simplicity.

The open plan further reinforces the loft feel by minimizing doors and cell-like rooms commonly associated with small beach lots. Spaces are defined by white, floor to ceiling curtains on tracks. Killen uses a honeycomb "Lexan" sheet material to define other walls in a translucent fashion. The kitchen is a collection of commercial kitchen appliances and stainless steel worktables on wheels. This fresh look gives the observer the feeling of the space extending beyond the walls.

Mixing traditional building materials and modern ideas about living, Studio 9one2 creates a quirky and striking modern house in a town filled with eccentricity.

Opposite Above Left: South deck off family room
Opposite Below Left: Asphalt-shingle façade at breakfast nook
Opposite Right: Main stair at third floor

Right: Main stair at entry
Below: View of family room with roll-up door to south deck from kitchen

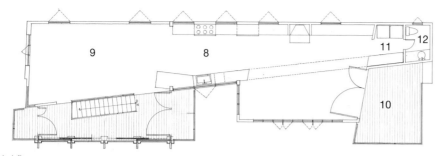

Third floor

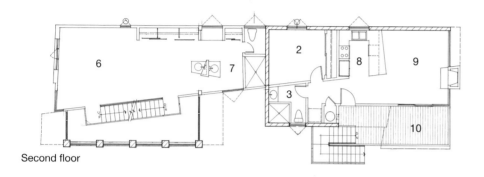

Second floor

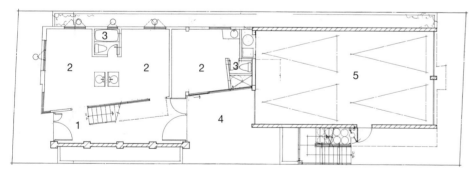

First floor

1 Entry
2 Bedroom
3 Bathroom
4 Patio
5 Garage
6 Master bedroom
7 Master bathroom
8 Kitchen
9 Living room
10 Deck
11 Laundry
12 Powder room

ANSELMO HOUSE

ANSELMO HOUSE

The 139 Hermosa Avenue site, is on a commercial strip, in the somewhat, less-posh side of Hermosa Beach. Its neighbors are a smoke shop, a Laundromat, a Sushi bar and a couple of cafes. It is also less than 100 feet from one of the prettiest stretches of beaches in southern California. Zoning allowed for one commercial space and one residential unit above, although the site could have supported more. Studio 9one2's task was to create an eye-catching façade on a busy street corner in a commercial district that served both a residential and commercial use.

Killen took his inspiration for this design from the original iPod. His solution was a blue mosaic tile clad tube that stretched the entire length of the property. The tube intersects a green plinth clad in solid cement board panels with aluminum expansion channels. Each end of the tube is capped with aluminum fascia and a custom-perforated deck screen. Asked about cost, Killen says the most expensive item was the screen, since it needed to be custom-fabricated. To enter the condo unit, one climbs a narrow stair to be greeted by a long corridor brightly lit by south-facing translucent windows. Killen didn't like the rooftop views of the adjacent commercial buildings. In the center of the main stairwell, is a large, rectilinear casework piece, which cantilevers playfully into the space allowing cutouts and counters for

BLENDING COMMERCIAL AND RESIDENTIAL ON A BUSY CORNER

BEACH POD

Opposite: West/ocean side elevation of residence

Right: Detail of perforated aluminum screen wall

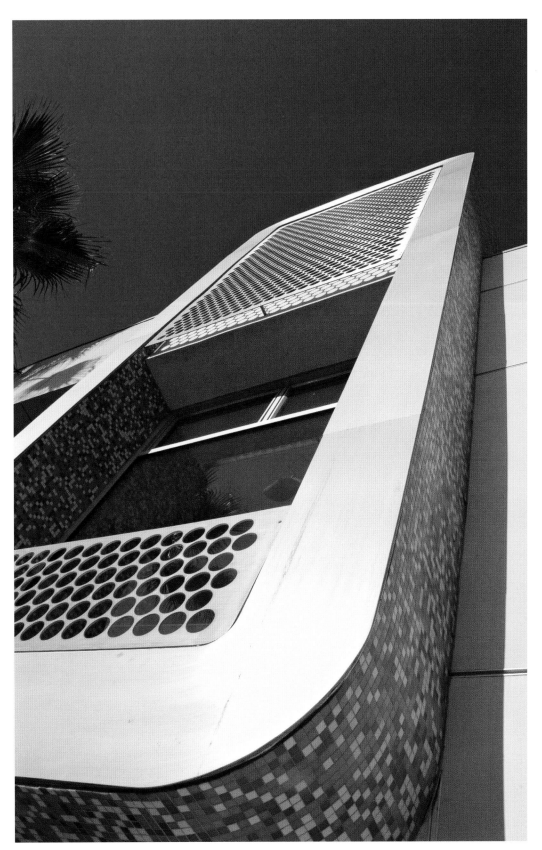

books. Climbing the stairs from the second-floor entry hall, puts one in the main living space, an open plan layout. Killen is not shy about built-ins. The fireplace surround is a large piece of casework canted at a 30-degree angle, from the wall and framing a huge flat-screen television. Adjacent to the fireplace is a cantilevered bench that sits comfortably under a window with a partial view of the beach and ocean. The condo unit lives on two levels and provides more than enough room for a small family and a few extra rooms for the owner's design studio. Logically most of the condo unit faces west and the ocean while the first-floor office faces the east and the last public street before the beach.

In a sea of eclectic buildings, derelict structures and trendy cafes, 139 Hermosa makes a definitive and welcome statement of modernism, regionalism and humor, which symbolizes the southern California lifestyle.

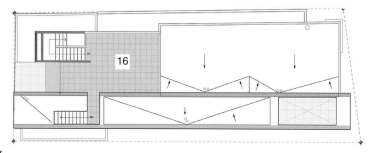

Roof

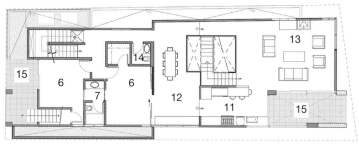

Third floor

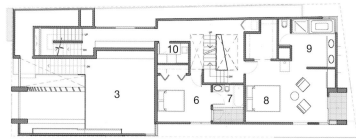

1 Residential entry
2 Restroom
3 Commercial space
4 Commercial parking
5 Residential garage
6 Bedroom
7 Bathroom
8 Master bedroom
9 Master bathroom
10 Laundry
11 Kitchen
12 Dining room
13 Living room
14 Powder room
15 Deck
16 Roof deck

Second floor

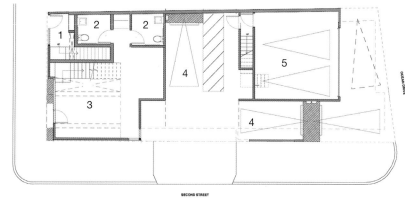

First floor

SECOND STREET

OCEAN DRIVE

Top Right: Shadow pattern of screen wall, stairs to roof deck

Opposite Above: Living room looking west
Opposite Below: Living room looking south

BEACH POD

Left: Studio 9one2 commercial
office conference room
Below: Stairway Atrium
Far below: Galley kitchen looking
west

Opposite: Primary entry façade night shot

Right: Ship-like curved roof form juxtaposed with angled "prow-like" mahogany balcony

The client wanted a house that was completely unique. They hired Studio 9one2 because of their reputation as Modernists and their ability to create "one-off" designs for their clients. Living next to the ocean, the client asked them to use ship motifs in the design.

Killen's answer to working on a very small lot on a Hermosa Beach, "walk-street" was to create a compact, ship-like house, with seven levels and two curved roofs. Fighting a height limit of 25 feet: Killen placed the ground-floor four feet below grade, creating room for a view deck on the top floor and a charming below-grade patio garden with water feature and fire pit on the walk-street side. The interior space is organized around a two-story living area with a southwest-facing glass wall, which allows daylight to penetrate both the main living area and the harder-to-light, north-facing rooms. Killen continued the ship theme with a canted deck wall and extensive use of mahogany both as exterior siding and interior casework and trim. The two-story window wall was also trimmed in mahogany.

The Croft house was filled with high-design features and clever motifs. Borrowing from Luis Barragán, Killen projects a concrete countertop through the glass kitchen wall and turns it into a garden fountain. The main staircase was an intricate weave of cantilevered mahogany treads interwoven into a slatted frame of mahogany slats and vertical steel rods. Killen took the mahogany

WANTING A SHIP AND GETTING A HOUSE

OFT HOUSE

THE CROFT HOUSE

exterior siding and brought it into the study repeating the inside-out and ship themes at the same time. The master bath had a custom designed stone tub and a wall of oversized ceramic tile, with a rusted steel look.

In the "Croft House", Killen blended dissimilar materials like mahogany and polished concrete with ship-like forms to create an elegant and sophisticated work.

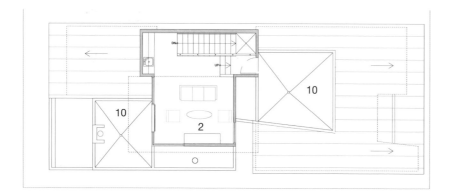

Mezzanine

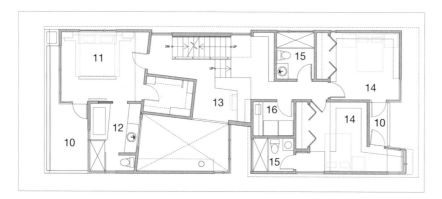

Second floor

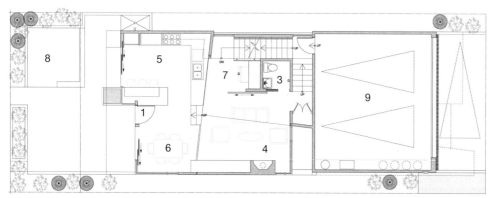

First floor

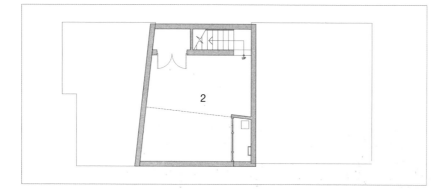

Basement

1   Entry
2   Family room
3   Powder room
4   Living room
5   Kitchen
6   Dining room
7   Homework nook
8   Patio
9   Garage
10 Deck
11 Master bedroom
12 Master bathroom
13 Office
14 Bedroom
15 Bathroom
16 Laundry

THE CROFT HOUSE

Opposite Right Above: Poured concrete breakfast counter with slatted mahogany cabinets below
Opposite Right Below: Water element extending through glass wall

Below: Concrete counter from dining room side looking east into kitchen

Left: Mid-level office/library adjacent to two-story living room below
Below: Master bathroom

Opposite: East entry/elevation

Below: Ocean views beyond in tight fabric of beach housing

The client for this house, was a sophisticated real estate entrepreneur, who had a history of working with architects and architecture. They were looking for an architect who could create a striking modern house on a narrow and steep lot. After interviewing some of Los Angeles' most "avant-garde" architects, they settled on Studio 9one2. This 3200-square-foot home, was designed to be their primary residence in a crowded beachfront block, filled with bungalows dating back almost 100 years.

Studio 9one2's design was to use the front and back height limit restrictions as an envelope for a folded plate design, which sloped downward to the ocean side of the property. Pairing a large metal clad form with a smaller stucco one, the net visual effect was that of a giant, 3-D paperclip. Inside, Killen designed a stair-stepping scheme of five levels that stays under the city's sloping height limit while creating views at each floor level. The garage, at the lowest part of the design, is separated from the balance of the building by a landscaped area, which creates a natural garden patio for the house. The internal circulation, is created by a glass-treaded staircase, which runs from the top street entry to the ground level, on the south and lower façade. This circulation module, painted deep red inside and out, runs the length of the house and gives visual access throughout. Killen brings light into his narrow building by

A PROW AT THE BEACH

RESIDENCE

DIESER RESIDENCE

Left: "3 Pier" cantilevered view deck
Below Top: Residence in neighborhood context
Below Bottom: West balcony off living room

introducing ample clerestory windows and glass plate floor inserts along the circulation module.

Having great ocean views is an essential design requirement in any modern beach house. Studio 9one2 accomplishes this in a variety of ways, with multi-story window walls and multi-level decks with glass guard-rails. The most unique feature, however, is a cantilevered deck that shoots out 21 feet from the west façade and offers unobstructed views of the ocean and all three local piers. The small view deck was designed to slide under the height limit and provides a view of the piers, which can only be seen from that furthest-west vanishing point. This steel and glass element along with the dramatic folded plate design, completes the composition of the "Dieser" residence, with a gravity defying "tech" look, which is in stark contrast to the quaint surrounding homes.

Below: Kitchen looking east

Opposite Above Left: View from living room through family room
Opposite Below Left: Primary stairs

Following Two Pages: Main entertainment spaces looking west

DIESER RESIDENCE

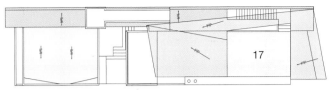

Roof deck

Second floor

First floor

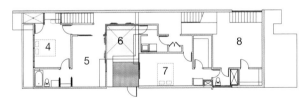

Basement 2

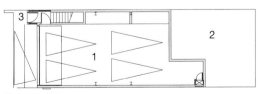

Basement 1

1   3 car garage
2   Storage
3   Informal beach entry
4   Bedroom
5   Study
6   Courtyard
7   Bedroom w/ bath
8   Art/Library
9   Master bedroom
10 Master bathroom
11 Entry
12 Living room
13 Dining room
14 Family room
15 Kitchen
16 Powder room
17 Roof deck

The client for this house was a well-known commercial glass fabricator. Having worked with many of Los Angeles' best architectural firms, he had an intimate knowledge of their skills and capabilities. He chose Studio 9one2 for both its design prowess and master-builder skills. Ettley was looking for an architect who could be creative with big glass and Killen was that person.

Sitting only a few blocks from the ocean, this tight corner lot asked for something dramatic. The client wanted Studio 9one2 to feature his company's commercial glass skills. Killen obliged with a house that is a study in solid-void relationships and a "glass showcase." Fourteen-foot-high glass bays pop out from a commercial window wall façade and are nestled under a huge aluminum and wood canopy roof. At certain times of the day, the floor to ceiling glass bays reflect the blue sky on the deeply tinted blue-glass and create the illusion of blocks of frozen blue Pacific Ocean. Interspersed with the glazed bays are bays of slatted mahogany that create a solid offset for the dark blue glass, creating the appearance of a modern seaside sculpture. Situated just a few blocks from the ocean, the ascending lot achieves commanding views of the water, while providing a cityscape foreground to the setting. The master suite, located at the mid-level front, had a glass floor

Opposite: Northwest corner view

Above Top: Twilight/sunset
Above Bottom: Master sitting room glass floor

A DRAMATIC REINTERPRETATION OF THE GLASS BOX

LEY HOUSE

Above: North elevation
Right: Glass and mahogany detailing

Opposite right: Vertical garden box out of mahogany, containing bamboo

sitting area, which overlooked a reflecting pond and garden below. This patio was located off the theater/family room. On the side of this master suite bay, Killen designed a bamboo garden framed by a vertical mahogany trellis. The bamboo grew up through the building trellis and provides needed privacy to the master suite and the main living spaces at the top level. This vertical garden gave a Zen like feel to this corner of the house.

Studio 9one2 is known for its meticulous staircase designs. The majority of beach houses in the Los Angeles area are designed as inverted plans with the living spaces at the top level, in order to achieve the best ocean views. As a consequence of this design rule, stairs were in frequent use by guests and occupants alike. With this in mind, Killen decided to lift a page from M.C. Escher and create a staircase reminiscent of his famous etching. He accomplished this by having mahogany steps march up to a square glass landing and then continue on the next

Previous Two Pages: Primary living/
entertainment area looking west

Opposite Above Left: Master
bedroom and sitting area
Opposite Above Right: Kitchen
looking south
Opposite Below Left: Living room
looking east
Opposite Below Right: Powder room

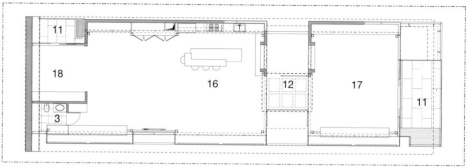

Second floor

First floor

side of the square. The effect was uncanny.
All that was missing was the upside down
scale figure on the top stair.

As in many other Studio 9one2 projects, the
outside treatments were continually being
brought inside. The roof soffit became the
ceiling of the top floor and was exposed
as wall paneling in rooms at the rear of
the house. Terrazzo, mahogany and glass
were alternately used as interior flooring.
The open floor plan with its giant glass bays,
soaks almost every corner of the house with
intense daylight.

The Ettley house is not for the private or the
faint of heart. But in a region, where being
public is very much a part of being, the Ettley
house is a work of architecture destined to
become a landmark.

Basement

1	Entry	11	Deck
2	Family room	12	Glass bridge
3	Powder room	13	Bedroom
4	Home gym	14	Bathroom
5	Guest room	15	Garage
6	Steam & shower room	16	Family-kitchen-dining
7	Laundry	17	Living room
8	Patio	18	Office
9	Master bedroom	19	Master sitting area
10	Master bathroom		

"The Gallenson" was designed for a lot with a commanding view to the Pacific Ocean, in the quaint beach town of Redondo Beach. The clients for this house were a professional couple whose hobbies were swimming and cooking. The husband wanted a lap pool for his daily workouts and the wife wanted a semi-pro kitchen for her culinary exploits. Since the lot was situated on a downward sloping hill with panoramic views of the town and ocean, finding a place for the pool and taking advantage of the view would require some creative thinking. Killen's approach was to bring the pool, the kitchen and the living room together in a unique way. He accomplished this by placing the pool immediately adjacent to the living room on the same level and having it run the length of the house above grade supported by columns. The pool sat 16 inches above the living room floor and was separated by a convenient bench. The south side of the house opened up with the glass wall tracking back 40 feet that exposed the pool and the view creating a remarkable inside-outside environment. The wife could cook in the kitchen while the husband swam laps and guests enjoyed the view from the adjacent living room.

Killen exploited the view slope side of the house by giving it wrap around window walls and roof decks with clear glass railings. He cleverly illuminated the street and upslope

SWIMMER'S PARADISE

SON HOUSE

sides of the house with 12-inch-high clerestories that rimmed the upper floor. He also used a glass railing on the staircase to give it transparency. To mitigate heat gain on the south and west façades, Killen designed a thin Mangaris-hardwood trellis supported by steel stringers. The primary bearing-wall that projected out onto the street level and formed one side of the "glass box" entry hall had a combed-finish stucco and looked like poured-in-place concrete. This slate-gray color and rough texture grounded the building by providing a visual anchor to what otherwise is a glass and white stucco building.

In the Gallenson House, Killen offsets boxy white stucco forms with glass boxes, masculine concrete colored wing-walls and hardwood trellises to create a subtle interplay of solids and voids.

Opposite Left: Suspended pool over spa below
Opposite Right: Night shot of pool adjacent to living room

Below: Bench along pool running length of kitchen and living room
Right: Retractable glass wall living room/kitchen, looking west

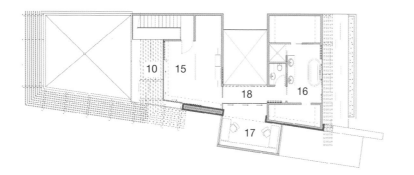

Second floor

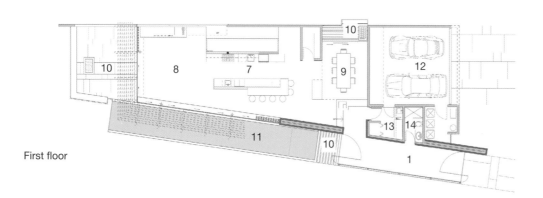

First floor

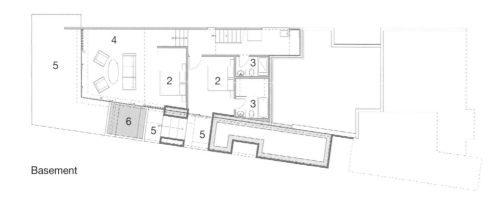

Basement

1 Entry
2 Bedroom
3 Bathroom
4 Family room
5 Patio
6 Spa
7 Kitchen
8 Living room
9 Dining room
10 Deck
11 Pool
12 Garage
13 Laundry
14 Pool bathroom
15 Master bedroom
16 Master bathroom/closets
17 Office
18 Bridge

Top Right: Primary living area showing south glass wall open to pool

Opposite Above Left: Pool
Opposite Below Left: Main stairs
Opposite Right: Dining room

GALLENSON HOUSE

Left: View west through kitchen
Below Left: Night shot of kitchen
Below Right: Master bedroom view
from deck

THE GLAZE

The client for the Glaze House, was a creative couple who were looking for an innovative architect who had experience in designing metal-clad houses on difficult lots. Studio 9one2 was asked to create a striking yet simple structure for this beach community home.

Studio 9one2's solution was to create a house composed of three distinct interlocking volumes, oriented on two axes. On the ground floor, two volumes align to the city grid; the garage, to the street; and an indoor/outdoor pavilion, to the exterior spaces. Ground-floor exterior spaces are connected by a path of concrete stepping stones set in loose rock creating a path that weaves from the street through the house and into the backyard. Between the courtyard and backyard, Killen created a pavilion enclosed by two glass roll-up garage doors, which acted as an entertainment space, when open and as a guest-room with a "Murphy" bed, when closed. This open space, also doubles as a children's play space; connecting the small, tight areas into a larger, contiguous play yard. The client's spouse, a horticulturist, worked with Studio 9one2 in designing lush native gardens, located at either end of the pavilion.

Studio 9one2 gave the house its distinctive appearance by placing a canted corrugated-metal rhomboid on the concrete block first floor. These top two-stories of the house rakishly cantilevered out over the ground-floor garage

Opposite: Primary street view

Above: Detail of west metal "box"

A SHINY METAL RHOMBOID

RESIDENCE

Opposite: Rear garden/play yard

Below Right: View through guest-room from rear garden
Below Left: View from courtyard looking towards rear garden

and pavilion. This corrugated-metal volume is rotated 12 degrees off the city grid: giving improved west and south light and ocean views from both the front, and back spaces. On the upper volume, Killen cutout the middle section, which allowed south light into the ground floor courtyard and the glassed-in circulation core. He added a cantilevered deck on the top floor to capture the ocean views. As an economy measure, Killen used

an off-the-shelf, industrial, metal stair system and then customized it with elegant hardwood treads.

The "Glaze Residence", simple in design, striking in appearance, makes a definitive statement on an otherwise ordinary beach-town street. It is an excellent example of Studio 9one2's imaginative treatment of simple forms and materials.

The Glaze Residence

Left: Living room looking south
Above: Kitchen looking southwest

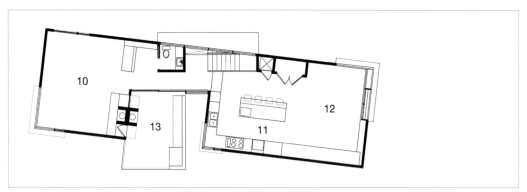

Third floor

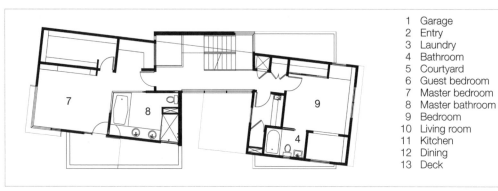

1 Garage
2 Entry
3 Laundry
4 Bathroom
5 Courtyard
6 Guest bedroom
7 Master bedroom
8 Master bathroom
9 Bedroom
10 Living room
11 Kitchen
12 Dining
13 Deck

Second floor

First floor

Top Right: Primary stairs

Opposite Right Below: Master bathroom

THE GLAZE HOUSE

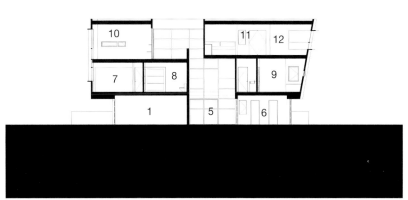

Section
See Legend opposite page

Herzberg was a restaurateur, who met Killen at a social event, where they discussed architecture. Killen expressed that "there was nothing better than having the ability to create your own living space." Killen's words must have had a positive effect on Herzberg, because several years later, Killen got a call from him to draw up plans for his house.

Herzberg's lot was narrow and long, and situated on the backside of a hill, in Playa del Rey. A major utility easement crossed one section of the property. That easement plus setbacks reduced the building envelope to a mere 70 feet x 28 feet. Killen's solution was to push the garage to the street's setback and the house into the hill. He then enclosed a large courtyard with a high wall with some very handsome cutouts and made that the main living and entertaining space for the house.

Because of its size and narrowness, Killen gave the house a loft-like feel, with an open plan first-floor and a two-story open metal staircase lit by a two-story window. The main living space flowed seamlessly into the main courtyard. The private spaces were located on the upper floor or on the mezzanine where Killen placed the master suite and office. Killen used redwood siding to clad the exterior of the master suite and cantilevers, the form over the first floor and into the garden, creating a ceiling for the sitting area below.

Opposite Left: Street elevation
Opposite Right: Courtyard with master bedroom in cantilevered wood "box"

Below: Detail of entry

A LOFT FIT FOR A KING IN PLAYA DEL REY

ERG HOUSE

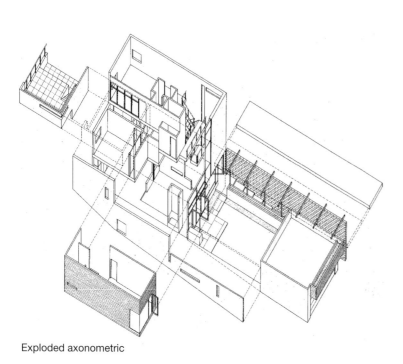

Exploded axonometric

Above Right: Night shot of courtyard looking into primary living spaces

Opposite Left: View front entry door to courtyard

Opposite Right: West elevation with cantilevered "ocean view deck"

HERZBERG HOUSE

He did the same on the street side to give relief to the intense whiteness of the stucco forms.

Killen felt it was important to create a dramatic entry for both the client and his guests. He accomplished this with an open-air two-story portico with steel frame and redwood-lined ceiling. One wall was an earth-colored sandblasted concrete block, the other was smooth white stucco. The two surfaces contrasted with each other and were carried through the house and into the courtyard. Killen did a similar textural offset in the flooring, with slate and hardwood.

There is always a careful balance in Studio 9one2's work and the Herzberg House is no exception. The overall plan is quite simple and almost loft like. But Killen's careful use of basic materials and obsessive detailing, gave this house excitement and made it a worthy representative of modernism, in an otherwise, architecturally homogeneous community.

HERZBERG HOUSE

Opposite Left: Looking down into two-story living space

Above: View from living room towards south courtyard
Right: Stairs at entry space

KARAMBELA

The clients, a young family with children, owned a lot on a "walk-street" in Manhattan Beach, that bordered on a large public park. Their goal was to build a house that mated well with both the park's imposing trees and the very public walk-street that it faced. Studio 9one2 developed a design concept to achieve a balance between private living and a public setting. The famed Manhattan Beach walk-streets were conceived as community gathering spots where you would go meet your neighbors. These front yards became semi-public spaces transitioning to private indoor spaces. Here the Studio 9one2 team placed the entertainment spaces at the mid-level with grand stairs leading to an opening glass wall that welcomed guests into an inviting and visually connected environment. Using a two-tiered entry and second-level deck, Studio 9one2 created an interactive setting for the young family to engage with their neighbors.

Killen used a large shed roof with a deep overhang to signify the house's park-like location and provide shade from the western sun. The ceiling and soffits are lined with weather resistant Koa adding to the "bungalow" feel of the house. The steel and wooden staircase is one of Killen's most innovative staircase designs to date. Killen designed "L-shaped" Koa treads and placed them on a notched steel stringer, in such a

A TREE HOUSE FOR MANHATTAN BEACH

S RESIDENCE

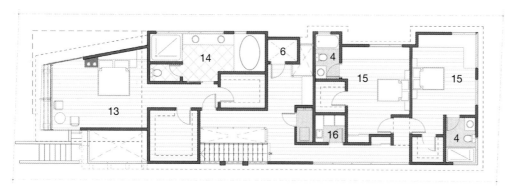

Second floor

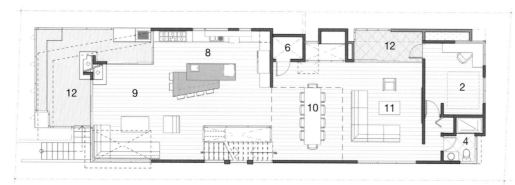

First floor

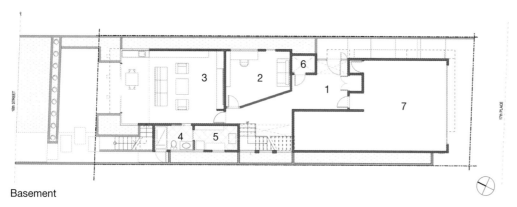

Basement

way, that they appeared to float upward. The adjacent window wall was filled with translucent fiberglass panels that give both light and privacy and add to the effect. The generous use of wood coupled with the stone and metal detailing created an almost *Zen* like feel to the interior spaces.

Manhattan Beach has gone through a significant building boom in the last thirty years and not all of it has been good. Some wealthy people built hermetically sealed "ivory towers" on their properties; these have run counter to the original intent of the walk-street designs. Studio 9one2's "Karambelas House" stands as a small antidote to that original intent.

1 Entry foyer
2 Office
3 Media room
4 Bathroom
5 Laundry
6 Elevator
7 Garage
8 Kitchen
9 Living room
10 Dining room
11 TV room
12 Deck
13 Master bedroom
14 Master bathroom
15 Bedroom
16 Laundry

Previous Two Pages: Living room/ kitchen looking north to walk-street

Opposite Above: Kitchen/informal dining
Opposite Below Left: Stairs looking toward dining room
Opposite Below Right: Media room at lower level

Left: Master bedroom top level looking north
Below: Wood and glass floating stairs
Far Below: Master bathroom

Sometimes, good things come in small packages. The "Lesman House" started out as a small package. The lot, 30 feet x 60 feet was the product of some odd property subdivision early in the last century. Bordering on a "walk-street" and surrounded by other houses, this lot had no vehicle access and consequently no garage. It was only buildable because of a grandfathered zoning rule that permitted it. Facing a walk-street on one side and The Strand on the other in Manhattan Beach, this lot was one of the most precious un-built pieces of real estate in Southern California. The client, Lesman, was a bachelor who wanted a showcase home in a high profile beach town location. He selected Studio 9one2 for their innovative designs and experience working on beachfront homes on difficult sites.

Studio 9one2's design approach was to create a space that incorporated ocean and beach views, as part of the living space. With a house of just under 1000 square feet, the design *parti* was driven by the need to create the illusion of more space than there really was. Killen placed all the public living spaces at the front of the house to capture the panoramic views and placed the private spaces within a series of concrete walls toward the back, thus establishing a strong connection to the beach and the ocean, just steps away. Two-story walls of glass stared brazenly at the beach and ocean while simple bush-hammered concrete walls

Opposite: Walk-street and Strand corner. North elevation.

Left: View from Strand north and west elevation

A JEWEL BOX BY THE PACIFIC

MAN HOUSE

LESMAN HOUSE

modulated the more private parts of the house and provided both structural support and separation from adjacent houses. Killen separated the house from The Strand and walk-street by placing it on a tapered dais and created a miniature front patio defined by a three foot high semi-circular fence. Killen designed an oversized roof cap with a weatherproof *Zincalume* fascia to give both a visual definition of the house's footprint and modest sun control. Incorporating the two themes of sea and sand, Killen used the building's colors and textures to remind us of what surrounds it. The sand color and texture was repeated in the bush-hammered concrete. The deep blue tint on all the glazing, controls the intense sun and gave the ocean a refreshing color, even on gray days.

Studio 9one2 considers this one of their finest works and numerous design awards have also confirmed this. Being in Los Angeles, the house is often the venue for fashion photo shoots and charity galas. On one of Manhattan Beach's most prominent corners, Studio 9one2 has created a "Modernist icon" that will stand the test of time.

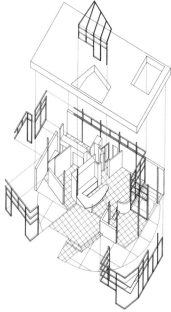

Exploded axonometric

Previous Two Pages: Night shot from the Strand

Above: Dining room view looking northwest toward Manhattan Beach pier

Opposite: Living room looking toward entry skylight and kitchen

Following Two Pages: Master bedroom at dusk

Opposite: *Main street view southwest façade*

Libiano was a commercial developer who had worked with Studio 9one2 on a variety of multi-family projects, before starting this house. He acquired a property for a single family residence in the prestigious and conservative community of Palos Verdes, with the intent, of building a unique home. After three years of difficult hearings with city officials, Studio 9one2 came up with a design that was a reinterpretation of the 1950's "ranch house", a very common house paradigm in all of California and something acceptable to the city.

This 3600-square-foot house used the ranch house format as a starting point. Putting *Studio 9one2* in a box, is a difficult task, unless it is made of glass. The design team's approach was to use a gabled symmetrical roof structure to frame a glass box that was ever so cleverly cantilevered above the first story. Here one could peer out at the neighborhood and catch spectacular ocean vistas. Killen supported his glass box with three huge beams that he extended four feet beyond the roof lines on both the first and second stories. In keeping with a more traditional home design, he placed the main living spaces on the first floor and private spaces above. The large glazed openings are framed in broad, oversized Mahogany trim, creating an almost lodge like feel for the house. However, Killen did not let his Modernist instincts be crushed. He gave the first floor a sweeping

REINTERPRETING 1950'S RANCH HOUSE DESIGN

ANO HOUSE

Below: Main entry with water element
Right: Night shot

open plan, with a smashing steel, glass and wood staircase placed right in the middle. Killen then added a shiny stainless steel fire pit at the entry and a Luis Barragán inspired fountain in the rear patio to complete his "fire and water" metaphor.

The Libiano House is an excellent example of how good architecture can happen even under the most restrictive environments.

LIBIANO HOUSE

Opposite Above: Dining and sitting room with main stairs
Opposite Below: Kitchen

Left: Master bedroom
Below: View to primary entertainment spaces

Left: *Street elevation*

The client for this house, was a creative couple with two children, who wanted to re-create the look and feel of a mid-century modern house, but within a new structure. They also needed to fit as much house on the property as they could with a constrained budget. Studio 9one2's solution used simple, inexpensive materials, wood accents and a clever, but uncomplicated design to achieve their clients' goals.

This 3100-square-foot house utilized the site's narrow eastwest orientation as it wove its way around a series of south-facing exterior spaces, which became extensions of the public living areas. These distinct outdoor spaces: the entry garden, formal courtyard, and rear patio, unfold as one goes down a series of interlocking steps that follow the site's subtle slope from front to back. The house's continual relationship to each exterior space was enforced through transparent façades and materials that created a seamless indoor/outdoor connection.

A simple material palette was used to define the various spaces within the house. The body of the house was stucco, which acted as a backdrop to the additions of concrete block and redwood forms. The concrete block walls surrounded and defined the most important spaces in the house. This concrete texture was juxtaposed with warmer redwood-clad

Left: Street elevation

A STUDY IN MID-CENTURY MODERN

panels that brought a soft and elegant residential feel to the project.

Reflecting the client's Japanese heritage, Killen integrated a number of motifs reminiscent of traditional Japanese design. The gardens were planted in a Japanese style, interior pendant lamps were take-offs of Andon, Japanese paper lanterns and the sliding glass walls, function in much the same way, as Shoji screens in a Japanese house. The design also integrated a variety of western design elements, such as, slatted steel railings, canted roof overhangs and projecting sun shades, which gave it a very modern American look.

With the "Sakamoto House", Studio 9one2 shows that good architecture does not need to be either expensive or complicated. Inexpensive materials and simple designs can be used to create an elegant building.

SAKAMOTO HOUSE

1 Garage
2 Entry
3 Laundry
4 Powder room
5 Dining room
6 Living room
7 Courtyard
8 Kitchen
9 Breakfast nook
10 Family room
11 Bedroom
12 Two-story entry
13 Two-story living room
14 Bathroom
15 Jack and Jill bath
16 Study
17 Master bedroom
18 Master bathroom

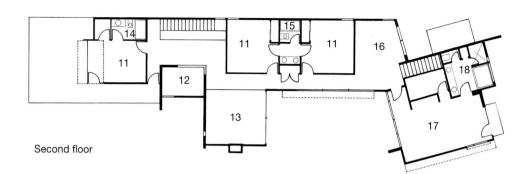

Second floor

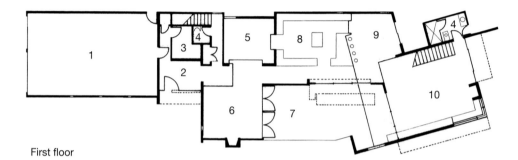

First floor

Below Right: View down to entry

Opposite Left: View from living room to exterior courtyard

Opposite Right: Second-level hallway near two-story entry

SAKAMOTO HOUSE

SAKAMOTO HOUSE

Opposite Above: Dining room
Opposite Below Left: Family room looking towards courtyard
Opposite Below Right: Two-story living room

Right: Master bathroom

The Shearin House is a seminal work for Studio 9one2. It marked a design breakthrough for Killen and put him on the map as the "leading residential Modernist" on the west side of Los Angeles. In 1991 Studio 9one2 was approached by the Shearins, a couple with children, who owned a beachfront property in Manhattan Beach and they were looking for a beach house that was "avant-garde." Shearin was a clothing manufacturer and had a taste for high end design. Killen's earlier work at the beach had given his client confidence that he could create the dramatic house they desired.

As with all beach front lots, the size and setback requirements presented a constrained building envelope. Killen's solution was to use the lifeguard stands, just yards away, as a design inspiration. He took the lifeguard stand's 78 degree windows and mimicked that shape by designing a canted fin wall that bifurcated the front elevation. Working from either side of this wall, Killen hung balconies and bays that projected rakishly toward the ocean. To add some visual excitement, Killen designed three large green glass sconces and placed them on the edge of the fin-wall. Internally, the wall was repeated in art glass and stainless steel, separating the atrium from the dining room. This art glass and stainless wall is also a water feature, which the family affectionately dubbed "Shearwater."

Opposite: West "Strand" ocean front elevation

Above: Sunset shot

A DESIGN BREAKTHROUGH FOR STUDIO 9ONE2

RIN HOUSE

SHEARIN HOUSE

Unlike many architects, Killen designs in three dimensions. Taking the 78 degree theme from the elevation to the plan level, Killen rotated the entire structure to a 12 degree, offset from the property lines and placed third-story balconies and bays at the same rotation. This subtle shift improved ocean views and separated the house from its close-in neighbors. On the main floor, Killen gave the house a grand curved staircase constructed of steel and glass. The steel frame was painted with an automotive finish giving it a durable and glowing look.

Using simple but durable materials, glass, stainless steel and stucco, Killen created an eye-popping, exuberant, Modernist building in a sea of sameness. With awards and press to follow, Studio 9one2's "Shearin House" established Modernism as a viable architectural motif on the western edge of Los Angeles.

Below Left: Entry
Below Right: Winding staircase

Opposite: View looking west from kitchen

SHEARIN HOUSE

Right: Water wall dividing entry from dining room

Opposite Right Above: Living room view southwest to pier
Opposite Right Below: Dining room

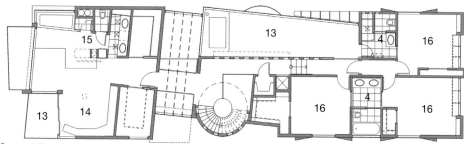

Second floor

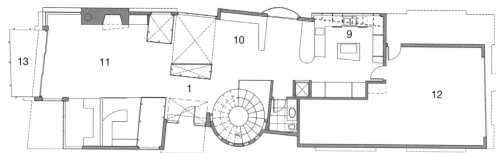

First floor

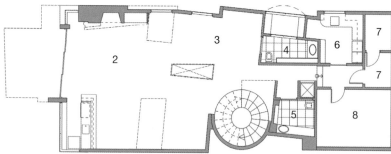

Basement

1 Entry
2 Family room
3 Exercise room
4 Bathroom
5 Powder room
6 Laundry
7 Utility
8 Storage room
9 Kitchen
10 Dining room
11 Living room
12 Garage
13 Deck
14 Master bedroom
15 Master bathroom
16 Bedroom

SHEARIN HOUSE

The client of this striking house was a professional couple, who both worked in financial services. They had small children and had admired other houses Studio 9one2 had done at the beach. They owned a larger lot in the hill section of Manhattan Beach that had wonderful ocean views to the southwest. The lot had a 20-foot level change from front to back, which presented both creative challenges and opportunities to the Studio 9one2 team. The client wanted an open plan design, which would maximize the view and have the look and feel of a Richard Neutra House.

Killen saw this as an opportunity to create a modernist-revival house, one that respected the terrain and took advantage of its level changes. He wanted to avoid the standard "layered cake" building design that is prevalent in this area of Manhattan Beach. By creating a two and a half-story entry and using horizontal and vertical integration of space, he opened up the interior on all levels. Studio 9one2 developed a modular pavilion style plan and was able to carve out a two-story atrium, which allowed all of the interior spaces to come together in a central gathering place. The geometries of this space was rectangular in nature with the exception of one angled wall, which sliced through the building, creating a circulation spine from the entry to the second-level rear yard. With views being a key design requirement, Killen placed

Opposite: Night shot

Above: Contextual primary elevation

A MODERNIST REVIVAL

ANN HOUSE

TIEDEMANN HOUSE

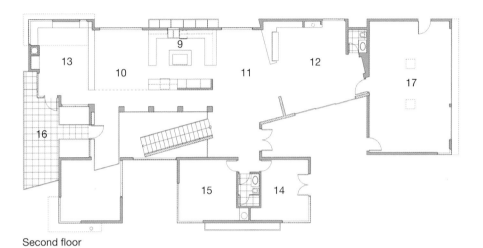

Second floor

First floor

1 Entry
2 Master bedroom
3 Master bathroom
4 Bedroom
5 Bathroom
6 Mechanical room
7 Guest bedroom
8 Living room
9 Kitchen
10 Dining room
11 Breakfast room
12 Family room
13 Library
14 Office
15 Gym
16 Deck
17 Garage

the main living spaces on the second level and bedrooms on the lower level. Borrowing design themes from Neutra, Killen created mitered-glass corner bays, recessed in stucco and wood overhangs. A better budget afforded the opportunity to use commercial window wall systems and recreate Miesian details in cooper and wood. An Eric Orr water sculpture was added to the courtyard. As in other projects, Killen brought some of the attractive exterior wood siding inside as soffit trim in key living spaces.

In a neighborhood of pretentious mini-mansions, the "Tiedemann House" is an understated modernist respite. Killen harmoniously integrates stucco, wood paneling, glass and steel to create a modernist string quartet for the eyes.

TIEDEMANN HOUSE

Opposite Above Left: Two-story entry hall and stairs
Opposite Above Right: View of deck looking northwest
Opposite Below: Dining room looking west

Below: Dining and kitchen looking east

TUCKER/V

Left: Principle street elevation

The client for this dramatic house was an aerospace executive and art collector. He wanted a house that had both exhibition space for his art and a house with some of the fit and finish of the extra-terrestrial objects that his company built. Once again, Studio 9one2 was asked to come up with a creative and dramatic house for a very constrained lot, just a block from the beach.

Studio 9one2 started with a grand entry hall in the center of the house. Here Killen wrapped the living spaces around this entry hall and added a spectacular glass, stone and steel staircase shaped like the "Nike swoosh." The steel frame and railings were painted with a Porsche Silver automotive finish, giving it a luminescent quality. On the ground-floor entry, he placed a giant, 10,000-pound concrete ball, which sat in a small entry courtyard outside that projected into the entry hall inside, where it became a fountain at the base of the ornamental staircase. The staircase hovers over the black reflecting pool and created a dynamic experience in the vertical circulation space. The entry hall was contained and illuminated by a blue tinted window wall that runs from the ground level entry to the top of the structure. By mixing in transparent and translucent glass panels in the window wall, Killen created both privacy and visual interest.

MAKING WAVES IN MANHATTAN BEACH

OLZ HOUSE

TUCKER/VOLZ HOUSE

Killen placed the large, open plan, main living space on the top level adding expansive windows and decks with views overlooking neighboring structures and a 180-degree Pacific Ocean view that extended from Malibu to Palos Verdes. On this level he wrapped a *Zincalume* metal band on the exterior that continued the deck line and curved it in a wave pattern to symbolically reflect the nearby ocean. Working with a better budget, Killen integrated high end materials, such as; travertine; *Zincalume* panels; curved glass with more prosaic structural steel; plate glass; and stucco, to create a dramatic house on a very restricted site. The house makes a strong statement, but Killen's artful interplay of form and textures soften its overall presence and give Manhattan Beach another unsung architectural hero.

TUCKER/VOLZ HOUSE

Opposite: Entry hall and stairs

Below Left: Stairs and reflecting pond
Below Right Top: View down to stairs
Below Right Bottom: Middle-level art gallery

TUCKER/VOLZ HOUSE

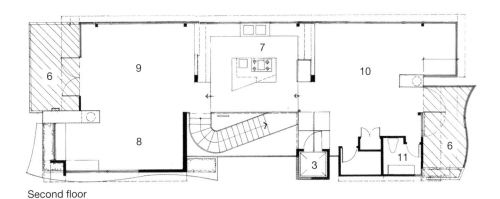

Second floor

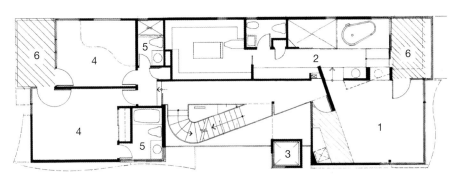

First floor

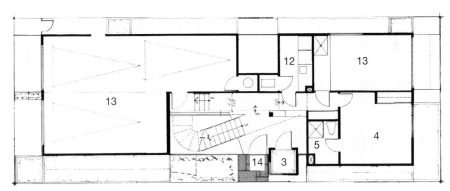

Basement

1	Master bedroom
2	Master bathroom
3	Lift
4	Bedroom
5	Bathroom
6	Deck
7	Kitchen
8	Dining room
9	Living room
10	Family room
11	Powder room
12	Laundry
13	Garage
14	Entry

Opposite Above: Kitchen
Opposite Below Left: Master
bedroom fireplace and television
Opposite Below Right: Powder room

Left: Master bathroom

The client for this compact 2100-square-foot house, was an entrepreneur and his wife, who bought a tear-down cottage on a small lot in Manhattan Beach. They wanted to build a house that would maximize their allowable building limit and at the same time, sit gracefully on the "walk-street" it faced. The lot, virtually half the size of a typical lot in the sandy section of the city, required Studio 9one2 to use every nook and cranny efficiently.

Studio 9one2's design approach was to exploit the lot's southwest exposure for both light and views. Behind an attractive patio of concrete planters and native plants facing the walk-street, the house rises up three stories, with a series of dramatic glass railed decks, offset by Brazilian-hardwood panels and Jerusalem-stone walls. By using a track back window system on each level, Killen brought the outside in and creates an illusion of spaciousness. In keeping with the "less is more theme", Killen brought the deck tile into the living spaces. This blurred the lines between interior and exterior spaces, thereby allowing the decks to seem larger when the glass wall was fully slid back. Conversely when the window wall was closed, the floor tiles met the wood floors and delineated circulation space from the furniture.

Left: Main street elevation

Killen anchored the stacked deck corner with a spa/pool on the ground level. The spool tucked neatly under the second floor

URBAN INFILL EXTREME
HOUSE

overhang giving the owners a cool, fresh-water plunge or hot tub on demand! Bounded on two sides by track back window walls, the spool and adjacent family room can become one outdoor room when the window walls are opened up. This space fronted on a walk-street that gave a community feeling while providing additional open space to enjoy the mild Southern California weather.

As with other beach town homes, Killen placed the public living spaces on the top level using an open plan design to create spaciousness that enhanced the ocean views. The Jerusalem-stone exterior was brought inside to clad the fireplace surround and accented certain interior walls. Killen used his signature cutout roof overhang on the top floor, to help define the building's edge, while adding to its openness.

Third floor

Second floor

1 Entry
2 Den
3 Bathroom
4 Saltwater pool
5 Patio
6 Garage
7 Master bedroom
8 Master bathroom
9 Bedroom
10 Steam and shower
11 Laundry
12 Deck
13 Kitchen
14 Dining room
15 Living room

With the "V2V House", Studio 9one2 once again shows that working within tight spaces can be an elixir for both creativity, economy and fun.

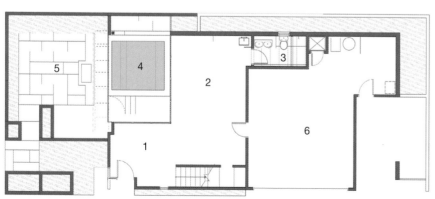

First floor

V2V HOUSE

Opposite: Stairwell

Below: View north to kitchen
Far Below Left: Dining
Far Below Center: Powder room
Far Below Right: Master bedroom

Left: Southwest building façades surround pool

Widmann, a real estate developer and amateur athlete, was a long-time client of Studio 9one2 and had worked with the studio on a number of commercial ventures. He assembled two full street-to-street sand lots in the exclusive Circle Drive area of Hermosa Beach and asked Studio 9one2 to do something architecturally clever with the tricky double lot. The design was to include a 25-yard lap pool and main swimming pool, a gym, meditation space, office, home-theater, separate guest-quarters, master bedroom and four additional bedrooms. The client also asked that the residence have the feeling of a resort.

Studio 9one2's design approach was born out of a desire to have the main building areas separated by what would have been the property line of the two individual lots. Killen wanted to maintain the neighborhood scale on the main street and allow a view corridor from the upper street to the ocean. He placed the lap pool on the property line to provide this separation and aligned its axis with the end of Hermosa Pier, creating a vista for passing beachgoers walking along the upper sidewalk. This view corridor was underscored by a row of Sabal Palms planted next to the pool and ran across the property front to back. He then tied the two structures together with a transparent glass bridge over the lap pool at the topmost story, which connects the private half of the house

A HOUSE IN TWO PARTS

WIDMANN HOUSE

Opposite: Night shot of front elevation and water element

Below: View under bridge connecting living spaces to bedroom wing with lap pool under
Far Below Left: Back elevation
Far Below Right: Concrete bridge over lap pool

with the public half. Although the total house had a large square footage (approx. 8000 square feet), the two separate pavilions reduced the overall massing and fit in with the scale of the neighborhood.

Killen uses upscale materials, such as, travertine and *Zincalume* trim on the exterior and travertine and exotic hardwoods on the interiors to give the house an elegant look. A significant budget allowed Studio 9one2 to design and build extensive casework and custom furniture for key spaces. In an effort to reduce exterior massing and provide some visual fun, Killen brought out travertine-clad wing walls and intersected them with metal clad roof overhangs and sunshades in an intricate fashion. Borrowing a theme from another architectural great, Killen placed a Luis Barragán waterspout that overhung the front entrance and poured into an illuminated reflecting pool.

The Widmann house is a balance of restraint, respect for neighbors and lots of architectural fun.

1 Entry
2 Bedroom
3 Bathroom
4 Laundry
5 Study
6 Media room
7 Powder room
8 Kitchen
9 Breakfast room
10 Dining room
11 Living room
12 Family room
13 Patio
14 Lap pool
15 Gym room
16 Master bedroom
17 Master bathroom
18 Deck

Second floor

First floor

Basement

WIDMANN HOUSE

Opposite Right: Two-story living room

Right: Glass bridge
Below Left: Dining room
Below Right: Family room

Above: Kitchen/breakfast bar

Opposite Left: Skylight over stone staircase
Opposite Far Right Above: Master bedroom
Opposite Far Right Below: Master bathroom

WIDMANN HOUSE

The client for this breathtaking Malibu house was an entrepreneur, real estate developer and tri-athlete. He purchased this 2.2-acre site along the Malibu coastline with the desire to build a "trophy home"; a home with exceptional views, framed by exceptional architecture. The only drawback of the site was a major seismic fault line, which ran right through the property. Most coastal Californians live within striking distance of major fault lines, but few actually live right on top of them. Not to be deterred, Killen set out to use the very unstable nature of the land as a stepping off point for his design.

Killen's design placed an inverted gable roof on a series of canted walls and framed main living spaces on the ocean side with two-story window walls. Since the house was built on a fairly steep slope, Killen designed a long, see-through glass bridge from the entry into the main living space creating a *Piranesian* sense of drama. The main living spaces overlook an enormous lap pool, a preternaturally green lawn and the Pacific Ocean a few hundred yards away. The inverted gable roof stretched from three, to as much as, eight feet beyond the wall line creating a natural shade for the strong afternoon sun. It also became a rain catcher funneling rainwater into an underground cistern to be used later for landscape irrigation. Significant rigid steel framing and poured-in-place concrete buttressing provided

Left: South view of the ocean side façade

ON A FAULT LINE

RESIDENCE

resistance to any potential seismic event. The exterior stucco walls were painted in sand colored hues mimicking the beach just steps away. Sitting by the pool, one can enjoy the spectacular and uncompromising view of the ocean and remember that Malibu was a place long before it was the eponymous automobile.

Above Left: Glass wall and fireplace
Above Right: Butterfly roof detail

Opposite: Night shot of home adjacent to pool

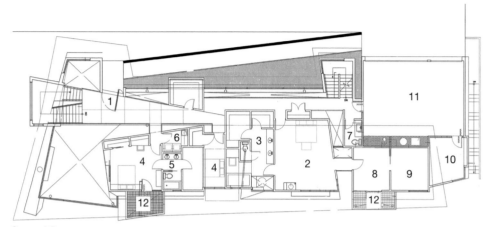

Second floor

First floor

1 Entry
2 Master bedroom
3 Master bathroom
4 Bedroom
5 Bathroom
6 Laundry
7 Powder room
8 Meditation room
9 Yoga room
10 Office
11 Garage
12 Deck
13 Great room
14 Kitchen
15 Dining room
16 Theater room
17 Gym
18 Gallery

Opposite: Glass floor at entry over great room

WIDMANN RESIDENCE

WIDMANN RESIDENCE

Opposite: Two-story great room

Above Left: Kitchen
Above Right: Dining room with glass
floor above

PATRICK J

Patrick Killen is one of the leading residential-modernist architects on Los Angeles' west side. His award winning designs are the synthesis of Bauhaus principles and Californian exuberance. Each project is infused with originality, cleverness and wit. He is constantly pushing his designs to the material and aesthetic limits creating architecture of remarkable beauty.

Killen grew up in the gritty steel towns of northeastern Ohio in a working class Roman-Catholic family. He went from parochial school misfit to collegiate standout at Kent State University in Kent, Ohio majoring in architecture. He migrated to California in 1980 and began his career with Skidmore Owings and Merrill, Los Angeles (SOM). After a short apprenticeship at SOM, he started his own firm, Architrave, in downtown Los Angeles in the mid-1980s. Weathering the challenging recession of the early 1990s, he re-established his firm as Studio 9one2,

the eponymous name of his Manhattan Beach address. Since that time he has designed scores of residences and numerous multi-family projects for a variety of Angelinos catering to their eccentric needs and desires. His strong knowledge of metal fabrication and material qualities has afforded him an edge in the sophisticated use of steel, aluminum and glass in his architecture. His work can be defined by its strong geometries, bright colors and fine metal and glass detailing.

Patrick John Killen is one of a handful of brilliant Los Angeles based architects that make significant contributions to the city's fabric and function; just below the radar of popular culture and universal recognition. Over the past 20 years, he has worked to transform the sleepy beachside hamlets of Los Angeles into one of the world's vanguard locales of architectural innovation.

OHN KILLEN

HONORS

2007
A.I.A. Merit Award
Paws a While Mixed Use Project

2005
A.I.A. Merit Award
Dieser Residence

1st Place 9/11 Memorial Competition
Manhattan Beach, CA

2003
A.I.A. Citation Award
Sakamoto Residence

A.I.A. Merit Award
Glaze Residence

2001
A.I.A. Merit Award
Sketchers U.S.A. Office Building

A.I.A. Merit Award
Widmann Residence

A.I.A. Merit Award
Anselmo Residence

1999
A.I.A. Citation Award
Herzberg Residence

A.I.A. Citation Award
Good Stuff Restaurant

Business Week / Architectural Record Award
La Marina Preschool

1997
A.I.A. Honor Award
La Marina Preschool

A.I.A. Citation Award
Lesman Residence

1995
A.I.A. Citation Award
Hamilton-Gregg Brew Works

A.I.A. Citation Award
Weber Residence

1992
City Of Hermosa Beach
Outstanding Multi-Family Award
First & Ardmore Condominiums

1991
City Of Manhattan Beach
Outstanding Commercial Award
1401 Highland Avenue

1990
A.I.A. Merit Award
A.A.F. Rose Bowl Aquatic Center

Concrete Institute
Outstanding Recreational Facility
A.A.F. Rose Bowl Aquatic Center

A.I.A. Honor Award
Architects/Studio Space

1988
A.I.A. Citation Award
Lee Residence

A.I.A. Honor Award
Manhattan Coolers Restaurant
Sherman Oaks

1977
Kent University
A.I.A. Student Gold Medalist
Henry Adams Award

& AWARDS

Russell Abraham

Peter Andreas

Charles Chesnut

Laura Hull

Brian Jones

Aaron Killen

Robert Millar

Dean Pappas

Holly Stickley

Adrian Tiemens

PHOTO
CREDITS